HEATHER WHITESTONE

Books in the Today's Heroes Series

A.C. Green
Andre Dawson
Becky Tirabassi
Ben Carson
Billy Graham
Chuck Colson
Colin Powell
Dave Dravecky
Dave Johnson
David Robinson
Dennis Byrd
Heather Whitestone
John Perkins
Joni's Story
Kay James

HEATHER WHITESTONE

by Daphne Gray
with Gregg Lewis

ZondervanPublishingHouse
Grand Rapids, Michigan

A Division of HarperCollinsPublishers

Requests for information should be addressed to:

ZondervanPublishingHouse
Grand Rapids, Michigan 49530

Library of Congress Cataloging-in-Publication Data

Gray, Daphne, 1946–
     Heather Whitestone / Daphne Gray with Gregg Lewis.
        p. cm.—(Today's heroes)
     Condensed version of: Yes, you can, Heather by Daphne Gray,
      Summary: Presents the life of the first woman to win the Miss
America title while suffering from a physical disability.
     ISBN 0-310-20457-7 (softcover)
     1. Whitestone, Heather—Juvenile literature. 2. Beauty
contestants—United States—Biography—Juvenile literature. 3.
Women, Deaf—United States—Biography—Juvenile literature. 4.
Miss America Pageant, Atlantic City, N.J.—United States—Juvenile
literature. [1. Whitestone, Heather. 2. Beauty contestants. 3. Deaf. 4.
Physically handicapped. 5. Women—Biography. 6. Miss America
Pageant, Atlantic City, N.J.] I. Lewis, Gregg A. II. Title III. Series.

Edited by Lori J. Walburg
Cover design by Mark Veldheer
Cover illustration by Patrick Kelley
Interior illustrations by Gloria Oostema

Printed in the United States of America

---

97 98 99 00 01 02 /❖ DH/ 11 10 9 8

Contents

Foreword 7

Chronology of Events 9

1. There She Is, Miss America! 13

2. Please Don't Let Her Die! 19

3. Profoundly Deaf 27

4. Say Drink! 37

5. Little Ballerina 45

6. A Special School 56

7. High School Years 63

8. The Choice 69

9. Miss JSU 81

10. First Runner-Up 92

11. A Dream Come True 103

12. Anything Is Possible! 117

Foreword

The first time I stood on the stage in Atlantic City and looked out over the empty convention hall, I was amazed not at its size, but at the fact that I was there. The journey to the Miss America Pageant in Atlantic City did not begin three years ago when I first competed in a local pageant. It began when I was eighteen months old. Even then, God knew his plan for me and how to make that plan happen. He used my parents to mold me, for I was too young to understand his dream for me.

This book is written from my mom's perspective on how she reared me and her feelings about the choices she had to make. In many ways, our family was the typical American family. We were not fabulously wealthy, nor did we have a prestigious name. We lived in a nice ranch house in a middle-class neighborhood. On weekends my father would often take us sailing. My sisters and I attended public schools, rode a yellow school bus, and had afternoon chores like most of the friends we knew. We had two working parents, family financial problems, and sibling squabbles. Despite my deafness, it was an extremely "normal" life.

I gave my mother my Miss Alabama crown soon after I became the 75th Anniversary Miss America because she spent hours lovingly and patiently teaching me to speak and to listen with the help of my hearing aid. I believe she is a role model to other parents across the country. On my national speaking tour as Miss America, I have met many parents who have deaf children. Many of them tell me how my mother gives them hope.

I often thank God for the blessings he has bestowed on me. The greatest of these is the strength he provided me to carry on when I wanted to quit and the dream he put in my soul when hope seemed lost.

What may come as a surprise to you is that you and I have much in common. If you can dream a dream, you too can accomplish it according to his will. God promises that "he who began a good work in you will carry it on to completion until the day of Christ Jesus" (Philippians 1:6). I pray that you will recognize the need for his help and believe in miracles from him. Hold fast to God's words and his strength through Jesus, and watch your dreams come true.

In Christ's love,
Heather Whitestone
Miss America 1995
John 3:16

Chronology of Events

February 24, 1973. Heather Leigh Whitestone is born in Dothan, Alabama.

September 14, 1974. Heather becomes sick and is hospitalized for two weeks. The medicine prescribed to save her life destroys her hearing.

December 25, 1974. After recovery goes a lot slower than doctors predict, Heather's family discovers something is wrong with her hearing.

March 1975. After months of exams and testing, Heather's family is told she is profoundly deaf.

Summer 1975. Heather is fitted with hearing aids.

July 1976. Heather, her sisters, and her mother go to Florida State University for special training.

August 1976. Heather's mom visits Porter Memorial Hospital in Denver and decides to teach Heather to communicate using the acoupedic method.

Fall 1976. Heather begins formal speech therapy.

Summer 1978. Heather's mom decides to enroll her in dance classes to help her learn to use what hearing she has to listen to the music.

September 1978. Heather begins public school.

Spring 1984. Falling farther and farther behind her classmates in language, Heather becomes increasingly unhappy.

Fall 1984. Heather begins three years of special schooling away from home at Central Institute for the Deaf in St. Louis, Missouri.

Fall 1987. After making up six years of academic progress at CID in just three years, Heather comes home to begin public high school in Dothan.

Spring 1988. Heather's parents divorce.

Fall 1988. Heather wins admittance to Alabama School of Fine Arts. She moves to Birmingham.

Fall 1989. Heather transfers to Berry High School and joins the Briarwood Ballet.

January 1990. Heather begins to learn sign.

November 1990. Heather wins second runner-up in the Miss Shelby County Junior Miss.

Spring 1991. After graduating from high school, Heather enters the Miss Deaf Alabama Pageant.

Fall 1991. Heather enrolls at Jacksonville State University.

Spring 1992. Heather enters the Miss Saint Clair Pageant and then wins Miss Jacksonville State.

June 1992. In her first state competition for Miss Alabama, Heather is named first runner-up.

July 1992. Heather is named Miss Point Mallard and qualifies for the 1993 Miss Alabama pageant.

June 1993. Dancing to "Via Dolorosa" for the first time, Heather wins the talent portion and is named first runner-up to Miss Alabama again.

September 1993. Uncertain whether she will run again, Heather and her mom attend the Miss America competition in Atlantic City.

November 1993. Heather enters and wins the Miss Cullman Area Pageant.

June 1994. Heather is named Miss Alabama.

September 17, 1994. Her dream comes true when Heather is crowned Miss America 1995.

1

There She Is, Miss America!

September 17, 1994. Atlantic City, New Jersey.
When Regis Philbin and Kathy Lee Gifford, television hosts for the Miss America Scholarship Pageant,
announced the finalists, the second name called was
"Heather Whitestone, Miss Alabama." I was never more
proud of my daughter.

As all five remaining contestants took their seats
for the interview portion of the competition, a hush of
anticipation settled across that vast convention hall.
During the evening gown competition, Heather had
been elegant. She'd looked great during the swimsuit

segment as well. Then for the talent portion of the competition she captivated the entire audience with her electrifying performance—a classic ballet interpretation of the Crucifixion danced to Sandi Patty's inspirational song "Via Dolorosa."

But the interview was the contestants' last chance to impress the judges. Each finalist would be judged on her response to Regis Philbin's questions. For Heather, these next few minutes were to be perhaps the most difficult and most unpredictable aspect of the whole pageant. My daughter's performance here would make or break her dream.

After asking Miss Georgia the first question, Regis turned his attention to Heather and said to the audience, "You may have read, Heather Whitestone, our Miss Alabama, is hearing impaired. No hearing in one ear, five percent hearing in the other. So I must ask you—you dance so beautifully—do you hear the music?"

Heather nodded and smiled. "I can hear some sound with my hearing aid. But what I do is feel the music and listen to the music ... for a couple times. Then I count the number with the music and memorize it in my heart. And that's how I do it!"

Then Regis asked Heather about the special program she designed to encourage kids to achieve their best. "All right, Heather, your program is entitled 'Anything Is Possible!' How can we remove the barriers that

limit us from realizing our full and unique potential, as you did?"

Not sure she understood, Heather asked, "How do we remove the barriers . . . is that what you're asking?" She had always been taught to repeat questions to make sure she'd understood.

Regis reworded his question. "How do you let people know that anything is possible?"

At that point Heather launched right into her answer. "My good attitude helps me get through hard times. And believing in myself helps me to overcome the obstacles. I have found there are five steps that can help people become successful. That's why I created my STARS program. Stars have five points. So I thought that would help people remember these five important steps."

"You think if it worked for you, it should work for them?"

Heather nodded. "Oh, it worked for me! See, I experience this every day. And it really did help!"

Applause rolled across the audience, and I breathed a sigh of relief. Heather had cleared her biggest hurdle. All those years of tedious daily speech therapy had paid off by giving her a chance at her dream. Now, as the remaining contestants answered their interview questions and the television took its final commercial break of the night, there was nothing left to do but wait.

Finally the scores were tallied and the judges' decision delivered. The envelope was opened, and Regis Philbin called out, "Fourth runner-up, Miss Indiana, Tiffany Storm." The crowd cheered. "Third runner-up, Miss Georgia, Andrea Krahn." Then "Second runner-up, Miss New Jersey, Jennifer Alexis Makris."

As the cheering subsided, Regis went on to say, "Here we are now. Down to two. That leaves Miss Alabama and Miss Virginia."

Kathy Lee now said, "One of you beautiful ladies will win $20,000 to continue your education and the other will win a $35,000 scholarship, plus the crown and the title of Miss America."

"Okay," said Regis. "This is it, everybody! Ladies and gentlemen, the winner of a $20,000 scholarship is ... Miss Virginia, Cullen Johnson. And the new Miss America 1995, Miss Alabama, Heather Whitestone!"

The crowd of 13,000 packing the convention center exploded into cheers. The bewildered expression on Heather's face told me she hadn't understood the announcement. It wasn't until Cullen Johnson pointed at her, mouthed the words, "It's you!" and then gave her a big congratulatory hug that Heather realized she'd won.

I never did clearly see what happened next. I could tell Heather was crying. I was crying. Heather's sisters were screaming and jumping up and down. My parents, Heather's grandparents, were shouting, and all Heather's cousins, aunts, and uncles cheered and applauded like mad.

Regis and Kathy Lee started singing "There she is, Miss America ..." as Heather walked down the runway and waved to the crowd. But all that her family and friends could hear was the sound of wild cheering, our own and everyone else's.

When Heather made her turn and strolled back toward the stage, I could see her searching for her family in the crowd. I don't know why she didn't spot us immediately; we were all screaming and jumping up and down. There were thirty of us wildly waving and flashing her the familiar hand sign for "I love you." When she finally spotted us she signed her love back to us, and we all screamed even louder.

Her dream had come true. Heather was Miss America!

2

Please Don't Let Her Die!

We expected Heather to be a Valentine baby. So when she finally arrived on February 24, 1973, I thought, *Well, it's about time!*

Heather was born at Southeast General Hospital in Dothan, Alabama. Her father, Bill, and I had agreed on a girl's name, "Heather Leigh," several months earlier.

Both of Heather's older sisters acted thrilled when we brought Heather home from the hospital. Stacey was three and a half, and Melissa was just a little over two years old. I had said to Melissa earlier, "You're going to be a big sister, Melissa. How do you think you will like that?"

She looked unsure.

"Do you think you'd like to have a little brother or a little sister?"

"No." She shook her head. "I want a pony!" she said.

"Oooh! I don't think Mommy can manage that," I told her. "If I can't have a pony, would you rather we have a little brother or a little sister?"

"A sister," she said. So at least Melissa was getting her *second* choice.

Both girls instantly fell in love with their baby sister. To them Heather was like a live doll for us to play with. Whenever I'd sit down to feed or rock Heather, Stacey and Melissa would sit beside me, feeding and rocking their own little baby dolls. And they loved to hold Heather or help take care of her.

Heather developed very quickly at first—crawling, walking, and talking earlier than either Stacey or Melissa. Of course, Heather *had* to develop and move fast just to keep up with her older sisters!

*   *   *

When eighteen-month-old Heather awakened with a slight fever on Saturday morning, September 14, 1974, I wasn't overly concerned. I figured she probably had a twenty-four-hour bug. So I settled down in a chair to cuddle Heather while her big sisters watched their favorite Saturday morning cartoons. But the longer I held Heather in my lap, the sicker she seemed to get. When I called our pediatrician's office, the doctor told me to bring her right in.

After checking Heather over, the doctor said, "I think we ought to admit Heather to the hospital right away." When we checked Heather into the hospital, her temperature was up to 103.7 degrees. The nurses gave her liquid Tylenol for the fever and started an IV in her arm. The doctor ran some tests, but they didn't show what was wrong.

Heather slept fitfully most of the afternoon. I pulled a chair close to her bed so I could hold her hand, stroke her hair, and wipe her forehead with a cool, damp cloth. When she'd occasionally open her eyes, I'd smile and talk to her. But she never responded. Her eyes looked glazed, as if she'd been drugged.

That evening when the doctor made his rounds he said, "I suspect she has some kind of virus. If so, she'll get a rash within twenty-four hours or so. Then her fever should break, and she will get better."

But the fever remained through the next day. I held Heather and tried to comfort her most of the afternoon, checking regularly for the first sign of a rash. *Nothing!* My beautiful little girl lay in my arms, limp as a rag doll. That afternoon, her only sign of life was that from time to time she would whine a little bit.

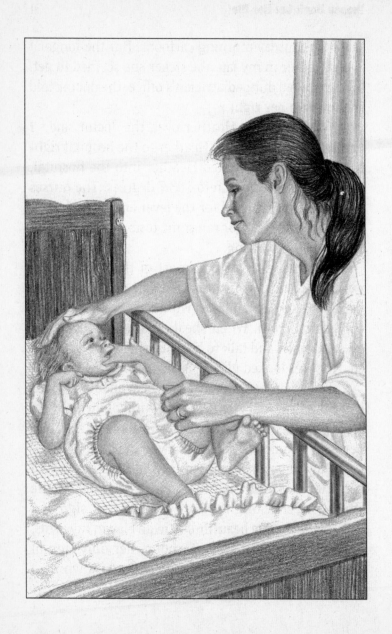

Monday dawned. Another pediatrician came in that morning and ordered more blood tests. "We should have the results of these back by Thursday," he said.

Thursday! I thought. *But this is just Monday. How long can this go on?*

I think that's when my mother's instincts began telling me, *There's something wrong here. This isn't right.* I felt even more worried minutes later when the medical technician who came to take blood from Heather said, his voice full of concern, "We have a mighty sick little girl here."

Heather's temperature climbed to 104.3 early that afternoon. And Heather now winced in pain whenever anyone lifted her or shifted her position in the bed. She was getting worse, not better.

Upon awakening Tuesday morning, I noticed a slight swelling of Heather's left hand and wrist. When I called the nurses in to look, they couldn't see it; they thought I was looking too hard for a rash. When the doctor came, he dismissed my concern just as quickly as the nurses had.

But I'd spent most of the past three days holding and stroking my baby's hands. I felt sure about the swelling. I wasn't imagining things.

Tuesday proved to be another rough, restless night. By 9:00 A.M. Wednesday Heather's hand had ballooned to nearly twice its normal size, and the skin had turned bright red. There was no denying it now. The nurse contacted the pediatricians' office, and two doctors arrived at the hospital about noon. They examined Heather quickly and then removed her from the room for "further blood tests."

Wednesday night was the worst yet. The doctors had removed the IV. Since she was no longer getting any nourishment through the IV, the nurses provided me a small syringe to try to force liquid into her mouth a few drops at a time. I may have managed to get her to swallow a little bit of liquid. But by this time her joints were so swollen we couldn't lift her or even turn her on the bed without her whimpering in pain.

Looking down at my little girl on that bed, I began to cry. I was scared to death I was going to lose my baby girl, and I couldn't even take her in my arms to comfort her without causing her more pain.

All I could do was pace—back and forth from one side of the room to the other—worrying, crying, and praying. *Please, Lord, oh please don't let her die!* I knew in my heart God was there; I believed he could hear me. But never in my life had I felt so frightened and alone.

By the time the doctor made his rounds Thursday morning, the swelling had progressed noticeably farther up Heather's arms. Now even the right foot had begun to swell. She had become so sensitive to touch that we couldn't even drape a sheet over her without making her cry out. Finally I told Heather's father, "I won't stand by anymore and just watch her die!"

With that I marched out of the room and stormed down the hall to the nurse's station. "I want you to get on that phone right now," I screamed at the startled woman at the desk. "You call our doctors right now! And you inform them that unless they can begin some kind of treatment for Heather or start giving us some answers in the next few hours, I'm going to remove her from this hospital and take her to Birmingham Children's Hospital, where I know someone will do something for my daughter!"

By 10 A.M. the nurses received the new orders. We were asked to sign a form giving permission for Heather to receive two shots of antibiotics. I couldn't believe I'd had to pitch a temper tantrum to make it happen, but at least something was finally being done.

I do recall thinking, *If we have to sign this, whatever they're giving her must be powerful stuff.* But even if someone had explained the potential dangers, I doubt we'd have made a different decision. I believed in my heart that morning that Heather was on the verge of death. Something had to be done—and soon.

Thankfully we didn't have to wait long for the first signs of improvement. By late afternoon I detected a slight reduction in the swelling. By suppertime Heather even managed to swallow the first few bites of food she'd had in almost a week.

Gradually I began to relax. After two days they took Heather off the more dangerous of the two drugs. But it wasn't until the end of the second week that Heather's temperature finally leveled out. By Friday the doctors said everything was looking good. Saturday morning they told us we could take our little girl home.

We were told to continue giving her medicine and to bring her back to the doctors' office for a checkup in about a week. They said Heather's leg, where she got her shots, would be sore, so she wouldn't be able to walk right away. But they said she should be running around with everything back to normal in two to three weeks.

The doctors were wrong.

3

Profoundly Deaf

Stacey and Melissa were overjoyed to have their little sister home again. They brought Heather her favorite toys, talked to her constantly, and tried to get her to play with them. Heather smiled. She touched her favorite stuffed animals. But she was too weak to talk or play.

Heather still wasn't walking or talking at her follow-up appointment the next week. The doctor said not to worry. "This infection won't go away as quickly as a normal virus or cold would," he said.

Two weeks passed. Heather's bruises faded away, but nothing else changed. She could not walk or even sit up without help. And she still had not said one word.

Finally we took Heather to another doctor in Birmingham where my parents lived.

Dr. Humphries was concerned when he saw Heather. "We need to get her legs loosened up and strengthened as soon as possible," he said.

"How do we do that?" I asked.

"Place her in a tub of warm water several times a day," he said. "Gently bend her arms, legs, wrists, and elbows. She has very little muscle movement now, and we need to get her using her arms and legs again."

I nodded. That seemed simple enough.

"She should take some vitamins to boost her strength," Dr. Humphries concluded. "And please bring her back in one month. I'd like to check on her progress."

After just one week of her simple therapy, Heather was actually trying to walk a little on her own. Her gait was slow, wobbly, and crooked. But to us it seemed like great progress. By the time Heather went back to Dr. Humphries' office the first of December, she was not only sitting and walking on her own, but from time to time she'd even try to run.

Dr. Humphries smiled. "Keep it up," he said. "And bring her back next month. I'll run some more tests then."

*   *   *

There seemed much to celebrate that Christmas of 1974. Every day seemed to bring Heather a little bit closer to the healthy little girl she had been just four months before. What a wonderful celebration the Whitestones planned!

On Christmas morning, the living room was filled with torn wrapping paper, empty boxes, remnants of ribbon, and new toys. The older girls went outside to try out their new roller skates on the driveway. Heather sat quietly near the Christmas tree, playing with her new set of brightly colored pots and pans. Her grandmother Gray and her aunt Stephanie had started collecting the clutter. I decided it was time to finish preparing for our big Christmas brunch.

I opened the cupboard to pull out my largest company-sized frying pan. Of course it sat under a big stack of other pots and pans, which I had to lift with one hand while maneuvering the frying pan with the other. I thought I had the pan free and clear, but when I slid it out, the entire stack of metal pots and lids tumbled from the cupboard and hit the kitchen floor with a horrendous *CLANG*.

I jumped in response to the incredible racket—and I'd seen it coming.

For the first couple seconds after the ruckus died down, the house seemed terribly quiet. Then I heard my mother calling from the living room. "Daphne, I think you need to come in here."

Something in her tone made me go, even before I bothered to pick up the pans. And the troubled look on her face when I walked into the living room told me something was wrong.

"What is it?" I asked.

She nodded down at Heather, who was facing the tree with her back turned toward us, still playing peacefully on the floor. "I believe there's something wrong with Heather's hearing! Stephanie and I jumped out of our skin when you dropped those pans. Heather didn't even look up."

"She's just playing so intently with her new pots and pans that she wasn't paying any attention," I replied.

My mother shook her head. "I'm afraid that wasn't it. I don't think she ever heard the noise."

"You must be wrong," I told her. To prove it I moved over close behind Heather and clapped my hands. Heather neither turned nor looked up.

It can't be! I told myself. Rushing back to the kitchen, I scooped one of the pans off the floor and snatched a big wooden spoon from a drawer. In the living room again, I stepped carefully over toys and around boxes until I stood directly behind Heather. Holding the pan tightly in my left hand, I banged the spoon against it with my right. *Bang*.

No response.

I smacked the pan sharply three times. BANG! BANG! BANG!

Nothing.

I leaned down right behind Heather and swung again with all my might. *BANG!*

When Heather didn't even flinch, I suddenly felt as if the very life had been drained out of me. I sagged to that living-room floor beside my little girl, who finally noticed my presence. Looking over and seeing the spoon and pan in my hands, she smiled sweetly and went back to stirring the pretend meal she was "cooking" in her toy pot.

I stayed slumped on the floor, staring at Heather through a blur of tears, asking God: *How much more are we going to have to go through?*

In the background carols played softly on the stereo. Neither Heather nor I could hear them. There was no Christmas spirit left in the Whitestone house that day.

*   *   *

Heather went for complete hearing tests at the University of Alabama-Birmingham's Spain Clinic. While Heather went through one exercise after another with an examiner in a tiny soundproof room, I prayed whatever problem they found with Heather could be quickly and easily corrected.

On the afternoon of the second day, the Spain Clinic staff finished their testing and called us in to a small conference room to give us a report. Several people spoke briefly to review what they'd done with Heather and the findings of their tests.

Then the chief audiologist summed things up fairly quickly by explaining, "Our conclusion is that Heather has suffered a severe to profound hearing loss in both ears."

"And what exactly does that mean?"

"Well," the audiologist replied, "we have found that with children like Heather, who are classified as profoundly deaf..."

Profoundly deaf? Heather's profoundly deaf?

"Help me understand what you're saying," I pleaded. "We've never had anyone who was deaf in our family. I don't even know anyone who is deaf. What should we expect out of a 'profoundly deaf' child? Give me a quick long-range picture."

"Well," the man began, "that's difficult to do because so much depends on the child, her family, and the education and training she gets. But I can say this: as a profoundly deaf person, Heather probably won't develop much verbal speech. Most children with her degree of deafness use sign language rather than speak. When it's time for her to go to school, she will probably need to attend a special school such as the Alabama School for the Deaf in Talladega. You can expect her to achieve maybe a third-grade level of education."

That report seemed so horrible it made it hard to listen to the other advice the experts had. But they said it was very important to begin speech therapy as soon as possible in order to maintain and stimulate any remaining speech Heather might have. To help with that therapy, they also recommended that Heather get fitted for a hearing aid to improve what little hearing was left. Because they thought Heather should begin language development as soon as possible, they also suggested Heather be taught sign language right away.

When I walked from the Spain Clinic to the bookstore to purchase a sign language book that afternoon, I was still in shock. But when I asked a clerk if they had any copies of *Signing Exact English* she took me right to them. I flipped through one of the thick green paperbacks. It reminded me of a massive picture book, full of line drawings illustrating different hand and/or finger placements for different signs. Under each picture was the written English translation of that sign. Thousands of pictures. Thousands of words.

As I scanned quickly through that huge book an entirely new thought hit me. *If Heather has to learn sign to communicate, that means we'll all need to learn sign. Not just her parents and sisters. But anyone who wants to communicate with Heather. Her grandparents, her aunts and uncles, her cousins, her friends will all have to learn to sign if they ever have hopes of developing any kind of relationship with her or even carrying on a meaningful conversation.*

The thought terrified me.

*   *   *

Because the experts at the Spain Clinic had told us to start Heather on speech therapy immediately, that became the first big goal. But when I went to our local speech therapists, they all told me, "There's nothing we can do for your daughter because she's not speaking yet. When she begins speaking, bring her in. Then maybe we can help."

When I went to the audiologists to ask how to get a deaf child to start talking, they said they couldn't help either. "We just test," they told me. "For speech you have to go to a speech therapist."

I was spinning my wheels and getting nowhere. I grew frustrated and angry—at the world, at myself, and especially at God.

Then one gorgeous spring afternoon, I took all three of my girls to a local park. Sitting on a bench beneath a towering pine tree, I watched Stacey, Melissa, and Heather out on the playground. I saw how naturally the older girls had learned to accept and treat Heather as if she were normal. Yet they'd already learned to allow for her deafness. When Melissa wanted to get Heather's attention, she didn't try to yell. She walked over and touched her sister's shoulder. When Heather looked up, Melissa motioned for her to follow. It all seemed so simple and natural.

In that moment, God seemed to speak directly to

my heart. "You're seeing what Heather can do. Now, it's time for you to stop feeling sorry for yourself! You can sit there being angry forever, but that won't do you any good. It's time to get up and move on. I am with you. You just have to trust me."

In that little city park I reached a crossroads. After months of anger and frustration I was finally ready to trust God. He would help us know what to do for Heather.

4

Say Drink!

After that day in the park, God gave me a fresh dose of determination. I thought, *There have to be answers somewhere—even if I have to find them myself! I'm a teacher. I know how to do research.* So that's what I did. I went to libraries and began to read everything they had about educating deaf children.

Heather's father and I also took several trips to the state capitol that summer, making appointments with anyone in government we thought could help. "How do we go about getting a special deaf-education program established in the Dothan Public Schools?" we asked. "Can you help us?"

Even though Heather was only two and a half years old, we knew how slowly government sometimes moved. We figured if we started now, by the time Heather was ready for school, we wouldn't have to send her away to school.

During this time Heather also received her first hearing aid. None of the aids that are worn on or in the ear were powerful enough at that time. So by mid-July 1975, Heather was fitted with a body aid, which she wore strapped in place at the middle of her chest. A cord ran up under her chin, where it split and went to each ear. Heather hated it. But while she still couldn't hear a thing in her right ear, the aid did seem to improve her hearing through her left ear.

All our hard work at the capitol paid off. That fall, Heather and six other children attended Dothan's new deaf-education class for elementary age students. Although Heather was not yet three years old, she attended the class for special preschool training five mornings a week.

*   *   *

That next year we learned that Florida State University had a special program for families with deaf children. So for six weeks that summer of 1976, my three young daughters and I lived in a motel room near the FSU campus where we all "went to school."

All morning the staff kept all three girls working

on Heather's speech therapy. Stacey and Melissa enjoyed the activities as much as their little sister did. Even our homework assignments became group projects. We'd all go back to our motel room in the afternoon and continue our learning. For example, one day we searched through stacks of old magazines, cut out pictures of animals, and pasted them on index cards. We used these homemade flash cards to teach Heather animal sounds and names.

Even though Heather was only a toddler, I had to make important decisions about how to teach her. The staff at FSU talked to me about those decisions. They told me what people thought about deaf education.

"Some people think that all deaf people should learn sign language only," they said. "If you choose sign language, you will have to pick between two different sign languages: American Sign Language (ASL) and Signing Exact English (SEE).

"But some people think that deaf people should learn how to speak," they continued. "If the deaf learn how to lip-read and to speak, they are able to go to regular schools and communicate with hearing people."

I soon decided that I wanted Heather to learn to speak. If Heather was going to live in the hearing world, her family's world, she would have to know how to talk. But if she only learned how to sign, then she could only go to deaf schools and talk to deaf people.

So finally we decided to check out a teaching

method called *acoupedics*. With this method, Heather would learn how to use the little hearing that she had. She would learn to speak, but she would not learn how to sign. If she succeeded with this method, she would be able to go to a regular school with hearing children.

I learned that Doreen Pollack, who developed acoupedics, was the director of speech and hearing services at Porter Memorial Hospital in Denver, where we were going to visit Heather's cousins that August. What a blessing from God! I called Porter Memorial to set up an appointment.

Our visit to Porter Memorial Hospital was exciting. What impressed us most were the hearing impaired kids themselves. We met and talked with several—all different ages. And what seemed so amazing to me was that we actually did *talk* with them. They understood us, and *we* understood *them*!

I knew then, without a doubt: *This is what I want for Heather!*

I was full of questions. How do we start? Where do we go? What do we do?

Doreen Pollack's staff encouraged us, saying there was a lot we could do as parents to work with Heather. However, they also recommended we get Heather into therapy with a speech and hearing expert trained in acoupedic methods. But they didn't have the name of a single trained therapist in the entire state of Alabama.

While that seemed to be a major problem, I had been so impressed by what I saw in Denver that I refused to be discouraged. Those children I'd talked with at Porter Memorial Hospital had given me a vision of Heather's future. *Someday, somehow, Heather is going to be able to speak like that!*

Again I contacted everyone I could think to call in our part of the state. The search finally paid off when I found Judy Harper, a young speech therapist right in Dothan. She listened to my description of our situation and agreed to take Heather. Judy had not worked with many deaf children, but she was a warm, compassionate person who was willing to learn.

Judy started by encouraging Heather to make typical baby sounds like *b-b-b-b-b* and *d-d-d-d-d*. From there she taught Heather animal sounds—*baa* and *moo*. Finally, she began to show her how to speak.

We explained to the teacher of Heather's deaf-education class that we didn't want her to use sign with Heather. She agreed to go along with our decision. But the teacher used sign with other members of her class. Heather was bright enough to realize the other children in her class were talking with sign. So she began learning it too.

The more sign Heather began to pick up at school, the more she wanted to use it at home and the less she would try to speak. After months of hard work just trying to get speech started, she was suddenly refusing to speak.

I will never forget the day Heather ran into the kitchen all hot and sweaty. She tugged at my arm to get my attention. When I turned around she gave me the sign for "drink."

I saw she was thirsty. But I prompted her, "Say drink."

She signed again.

"No, Heather," I told her. "No signs. Say drink!"

I recognized the you're-not-gonna-make-me look in Heather's eyes even before she shook her head and angrily signed again.

"If you want a drink, you have to use words. Say drink!"

Heather just stood there, gnawing angrily at her lip, trying to stare me down.

"Sorry. No drink then!" And I turned back to whatever it was I'd been doing.

When I heard her stomp out of the room I felt like the meanest mother in history. My heart was saying: *How could you do that? Your daughter is thirsty, and you won't let her have a drink. Why make such a big deal out of such a little thing?* I did some serious soul-searching those next few minutes before convincing myself: *If she's going to learn to speak, you have to be consistent. It's going to take commitment; you can't give in.*

It wasn't long before Heather tiptoed back into the kitchen and tugged at my arm again. Pointing at the refrigerator she said something I loosely translated to mean "drink."

That was good enough. "You want a drink? Good. Thank you for asking. Let's see what we have that you would like." Heather grinned happily, and I knew our big confrontation was over.

I think I realized then that teaching Heather to speak would be hard—for both of us.

5

Little Ballerina

In those early days, one of the main goals of acoupedic training was to teach Heather to use what hearing she had—to get her used to listening. Judy Harper, the therapist, would hold one hand in front of her mouth to hide her lips and ask Heather, "Where's the *red* crayon? *Good!* Now where's the *blue* crayon? No, listen! *Blue!* Good!"

Sometimes Judy would play a tape recording of a common sound and ask Heather to pick the match from a set of pictures spread out on the table. A ringing phone. A barking dog. A car horn. Eventually she would ask Heather to repeat the word. Phone. Dog. Car.

Board games such as "Candyland" gave constant opportunity for listening and language. "Heather's turn!" "My turn." "Green!" "Uh, oh. Go back!"

Speech therapy was hard work for all of us. Every night I'd go over the homework Judy gave. All day, every day, I repeated words and asked Heather to indicate she heard what I said, or I'd ask her to say the words after me. The repetition seemed endless. But if a hearing child has to hear a word dozens of times before she understands it enough to use it in conversation, a deaf child may need to have it repeated hundreds and hundreds of times.

Progress often seemed slow. But every new word Heather picked up seemed a real triumph.

Everyone was encouraged when Heather finally seemed to understand her name and repeated a word that sounded a little like "Heather." But then for the longest time she thought everyone's name must be Heather. She'd point to Melissa or Stacey or me and say, "Heather." We had to keep telling her, "No, no. I'm Mama. That's Stacey and Melissa."

I'll never forget another highlight in Heather's speech development. It came one night, when I was putting the girls to bed. When I tucked Heather in and said, "I love you," she smiled sweetly up at me and said, "Wuv oo."

It had been over two years since I'd last heard

those words from my little girl. I gave her an extra big hug that night before I turned out the light.

Before Heather started public school kindergarten, we wanted her to be able to talk a little and listen well. But Heather still had a long way to go with her speech. So that summer, when Heather was five and a half, I came up with an idea I thought might help. Since music was part of Heather's listening therapy, I thought that if Heather took a dance class she might learn to hear the changing pitch and tone of music. Maybe that would help her understand the changing pitch and tone in the human voice, so she wouldn't talk in the flat, monotone voice common to many deaf people's speech.

But first I needed to find a dance instructor who would be willing to take Heather. Searching through the phone book, I discovered there were only four dance studios in Dothan. I picked one and called.

"Hello," I said, "I'm calling to see about enrolling my daughter in your ballet class."

"Wonderful," the secretary replied. "What's your daughter's name?"

"Heather."

"And how old is Heather?"

"She's five. She'll be starting kindergarten this year."

"Has she had any dance classes before now?"

"No. This would be her first."

"That'll be fine. We have several openings left in our beginner's troupe."

"There is a problem I should tell you about," I said. "Heather is profoundly deaf."

The secretary was silent for a long time. Then she stuttered, "Well ... uh ... we'll need to think about that. I ... uh ... don't know how my instructor would feel about that. Let me talk to our beginning ballet teacher and get back to you. Can I have your number?"

She never returned my call. Neither did the next dance school.

So I called the third name on my list: the Dothan School of Dance. I went through the same conversation until I got to the part where I told her, "Heather is profoundly deaf."

"I don't think that will be a serious problem," the director said. "Let's give it a try and see how it goes. We'll look forward to having Heather in our dance class."

So we signed her up, and Heather discovered quickly that she absolutely loved to dance. She was soon twirling and dancing everywhere she went. Through the house. Out in the yard. Down the aisles of the grocery store. In her own mind Heather had become a prima ballerina overnight.

*   *   *

Kindergarten didn't go nearly as well. Heather

didn't seem to listen during class. When it was time to work on papers at the table, she would wander off and play in the block center. And when the teacher tried to get her to come back to the table, she would throw a temper tantrum. At the end of the school year, Heather's teacher told us she needed to be held back. "It's too difficult to understand her speech," she said. "And we do not think she is ready for first-grade work."

School officials said they were willing to try her in kindergarten again. But they really wanted me to pull her out of the regular classroom and put her back in the deaf-education unit. But I didn't want to do that.

So I prayed for guidance and called Dr. Haas, director of the rehab center, down at Florida State University. "We've got a problem with Heather and the schools here," I told him. "I don't know what to do."

*   *   *

The specialists down at FSU ran a number of tests on Heather. They found she had a vocabulary of 225–250 words. But the average vocabulary for a six-year-old child is 2,500 words! So she was way behind her classmates in language development. The good news came from the results of Heather's intelligence tests, which said, "Heather appears to be an intellectually gifted deaf child." The tests showed that, because Heather was highly intelligent, she still had a good chance of learning to speak.

With that report the school officials agreed to move Heather on to first grade. And her first-grade teacher, Mrs. Wages, did a great job of working with Heather. She made a point, when they had a spelling test, to sit right in front of Heather when she read the words aloud, instead of walking around the class. She also wore a little transmitter and spoke through a microphone. Her voice came through Heather's Phonic Ear trainer, an amplifier which boosted the sound for Heather's hearing aid.

Our combination of hearing aid and hard work paid off. Heather enjoyed school. We didn't frustrate the teacher. And Heather didn't have temper tantrums anymore.

Heather's second-grade teacher, Mrs. Sutherland, told her students, "In this room we are going to look after each other—like family." Quickly, her students learned to treat Heather kindly. When children from other classes made fun of Heather on the playground, her classmates quickly came to her defense and then told Mrs. Sutherland what had happened.

The kids would even interpret for Heather. When she didn't understand the teacher's instructions, children nearby would say, "This is what Mrs. Sutherland wants us to do," and explain it. And when Mrs. Sutherland didn't understand Heather, her classmates often did, and they would tell their teacher what Heather had said.

Mrs. Sutherland tried to treat Heather like any other child in the room. One day, Mrs. Sutherland sent Heather on an errand to get a book. It took longer than she'd expected it would. But Heather returned a few minutes later with the book and a proud smile on her face.

That afternoon after school one of the other teachers stopped Mrs. Sutherland in the hall. "Did you realize you sent that little Whitestone girl to my class to give me that message this morning?"

"Of course! What about it?"

"But she's deaf!"

"I know that!" Mrs. Sutherland laughed.

"It took me the longest time to figure out what she wanted."

"But you did, didn't you?"

The teacher smiled and nodded her head. "Only because that child refused to leave until she got what you wanted. She just kept right on talking and talking until I finally understood. I'll say this, she was one determined little girl."

Despite that determination and long hours doing classwork at home, Heather was lagging farther and farther behind her age-group in language development. So we decided to hold her back in second grade for an extra year to give her time to catch up.

Fortunately for Heather, she still had her dance. The rest of her life consisted almost entirely of hard work and long hours of speech therapy and schoolwork. Any progress in those areas came slowly and at a great price.

Dancing was different. For Heather it was pure joy. In dance class, students do not have to speak or answer questions out loud, so she didn't feel so different. She fit into the crowd and felt just like everyone else out on the dance floor. She believed she could dance just as well as anyone else in her class—maybe better.

Dance performances also gave Heather a welcome chance to shine in public. Relatives would drive from as far as Birmingham for her recitals. They always made such a fuss over her afterwards that Heather thought she'd been the star of the show.

Heather even used her ballet to tease her big sisters. On Saturday mornings, when they were watching their favorite cartoons, she'd twirl and dance right in front of the television. Stacey and Melissa would get mad and yell at her: "Get out of the way, Heather! Who do you think you are, anyway? Miss America or something?"

We used Heather's love of dance to develop her speech and reading skills as well. Heather never got tired of reading or talking about dance, so we checked out every book we could find about dance or ballet. We would read and talk about the books together.

In her second year of second grade, Heather continued to do well in math. And she did pretty well in subjects like science, because she had a good memory for facts. But when she was tested again at the end of the year, Heather actually scored lower on the reading segment than she had the year before. We began to be very worried. Would Heather ever learn to read and speak like a hearing person?

*   *   *

Fourth grade, the 1983–84 school year, brought a major turning point in all our lives. One day Heather came home from school crying.

"What's wrong, honey?" I wanted to know.

"Other kids not like me. Not be friends," she sobbed. "Because Heather different. I deaf."

I felt awful. I had known this would happen eventually. But it still hurt.

"You know, Heather," I told her. "Every one of us is different. Every person in your class is different. And God didn't make any of us perfect; the only perfect person in the history of the world was Jesus. Everyone else—all of us—have handicaps. Some are more obvious than others—like your deafness. But many of us have handicaps people can't see. Maybe we're shy or afraid. Maybe we're hateful and mean toward others. And if there are some people in your class who don't like you and don't want to be your friend just because you are deaf, then maybe that's their handicap. If it is, I think that's a lot bigger handicap than not being able to hear like other people."

Perhaps Heather was finally old enough to realize how different she was from the other children. Maybe she was tired of doing schoolwork every night until ten or eleven o'clock. Whatever the reason, she was discouraged and frustrated. To make matters worse, the school officials were pressuring the family again. They wanted us to put Heather in a deaf-education program.

Everything came to a head the day Heather came home from school with a library book. "You got a new library book today, Heather?" I asked her.

Heather eagerly showed me her book—a picture story about a little girl. "She like me," Heather pointed. "She deaf, too."

"It's the story of a deaf girl?"

"Yes. She dance like me."

"I see. There she is practicing her ballet." The little girl was like Heather, and I could see why she seemed so excited about this book.

Heather turned the page. "But she go special school. Just deaf children."

"She goes to a special deaf school, does she?" I repeated.

Heather nodded. Then she looked up and said to me, "Heather need go special school."

"Oh, no, Heather," I said matter-of-factly. "You don't have to go to a special deaf school. You can go to a regular school and live at home with Melissa and Stacey and Dad and me. I'd miss you if you had to go away to a special school."

I thought I saw a little disappointment in Heather's eyes. And that bothered me. From the very beginning everyone had told me that teaching Heather to speak would be the hardest and slowest way to go. For eight long, difficult years I'd been heartened by Heather's own bulldog stubbornness and determination to learn to speak. But if she wanted to give up speech, if she wanted to learn sign, I couldn't stand in her way.

I still believed we'd done the right thing. I was certain that God had been leading us. But I was suddenly overcome by doubt.

Even Heather now thinks she needs to go to a special school. What if I've been wrong all along?

6

A Special School

Once again I called Dr. Haas at Florida State University. This time he put us in touch with another expert who recommended we take Heather to the Central Institute for the Deaf (CID), a world-renowned school in St. Louis, Missouri. I called CID immediately and made arrangements with the school's director, Dr. Jean Moog, for us to take Heather to St. Louis for evaluation.

"We want to know what you would recommend for Heather's education. We're not really interested in enrolling our daughter in a special school," I explained. "But just out of curiosity, how much does it cost to send a child to CID?"

She told me the tuition, room, and board for resident students came to $9,500 a year. I hung up the phone in shock, saying, "There's certainly no way we could ever afford that!"

While *I* understood that, I don't think *Heather* did. Although we explained that the purpose of our trip was to test her to help know what to do about her education, Heather got it in her mind we were going to see a "special school," like in the book.

"Heather go special school," she insisted. Nothing else seemed to sink in. She got so excited on the drive to St. Louis that her father and I decided to let it drop until later.

CID *was* impressive. Everything seemed so carefully planned out. The classes were small— many had only three or four students per teacher. A child working in a third-grade reading book who was strong in math might be in a fifth-grade arithmetic class. They gave help where students needed it and challenged them in areas where they were strong.

I was also impressed that everywhere students went, they were expected to speak clearly in complete sentences. If a math teacher asked a student, "What is 6 times 7?" the student could not simply answer, "42." He couldn't even respond, "The answer 42." He had to say, "The answer is forty-two." At lunch students were not allowed to ask for "salt and pepper!" They had to say, "Please pass the salt and pepper."

But the tests Heather took at CID were discouraging. They proved how far behind she was in her language. The low point came when Heather saw a picture of bacon strips and called them "pig." At eleven years old, she didn't know the word "bacon," wasn't able to tell the examiner that the sun set in the "west," and couldn't answer other simple questions that a child her age would know.

When the testing was concluded, the Central Institute for the Deaf's director told us, "Heather needs to learn in a setting that emphasizes language and speech twenty-four hours a day. I think that here at CID she could make up lost ground. And if she did well here, she could probably go to a regular high school. If you are worried about the cost, there might be some scholarships available to help pay the tuition to CID."

"We'll have to think about it," we told the director.

But Heather had already made up her mind. "That where I go school," she told us all the way home. "Need special school. I like school. Feel home there."

"But it's so far away, Heather," her father said. "And you're only eleven years old."

She begged him: "Please, Daddy! Please! I need go there!"

Melissa and Stacey sided with their sister. "It's a good school," they said.

Finally, we decided to send Heather to CID. We

shopped for new school clothes and stocked up on toothpaste and other personal things. Melissa, Stacey, and Heather's aunt Stephanie had great fun helping Heather decide what toys and stuffed animals she should take. Through it all, Heather was really excited, so we got excited too. And that way we didn't worry so much.

All too soon we were in St. Louis, unloading the station wagon and getting Heather situated in her room.

Just before we left, I hugged and kissed her. I didn't want her to see me cry, but I think she saw how upset we were. "I fine. I happy. Do not worry," she told us.

Still we cried most of the way home.

Finally Thanksgiving came and Heather arrived home for her first visit. She talked and talked all weekend long. Remembering how frustrated she was last year in fourth grade, I was thrilled at her obvious happiness at CID. I knew we'd done the right thing.

She told us about her classes and her friends and about dorm life and her favorite teachers. All of us listened and asked questions and laughed at Heather's stories.

The funniest story she told involved an audio-trainer, the microphone and amplification transmitter which every CID instructor wore.

Heather laughingly recalled the day one of her

teachers assigned a few minutes of desk work and excused himself from the classroom for a few minutes. He'd been gone only a short while when Grace Lee, Heather's Korean-Canadian roommate, lifted her eyes from her work and looked toward the windows with a funny expression on her face.

"I hear rain," she said, obviously puzzled to see clear skies outside.

Heather and the other student in the class, a boy about Heather's age, looked at each other and grinned.

"What's so funny?" Grace asked. "Do you hear the rain?"

"That is not rain," the boy told her as he and Heather began to snicker.

"Then what . . ."

Just then all three of the students heard a clearly amplified flushing sound. "Oh!" Grace exclaimed as she finally understood.

A couple of minutes later the instructor returned to the room. "I thought I heard rain," Grace greeted him as he walked through the doorway. "Then I hear flushing sound."

With a horrified look the teacher glanced down at his belt. Yes, he had forgotten to turn off the trainer before he went to the bathroom. "The teacher so embarrassed!" Heather told us. "His face turn bright red!"

We all laughed for a long time over that one.

One of the best things about CID was that, for

the first time in her life, Heather felt as if she belonged. She felt accepted by her classmates, and she was very popular.

Theresa, the dorm mother, reported that Heather was a sweet and cooperative child. But she did laughingly add that Heather had a way of making it known when she didn't want to do some chore. I said that didn't surprise me; Heather had been stubborn all her life. Theresa told me Heather seemed to get along well with everyone. And she also remarked on Heather's spiritual sensitivity and devotion; she said there were several times when she'd walked into Heather's room to find her reading her Bible.

The CID staff affectionately referred to Heather as their "Southern Belle" because they said she had a Southern accent. I had to laugh at that. In all our years of speech therapy, I'd never thought Heather had any kind of accent at all.

Heather became best friends with Bola, one of CID's international students and the daughter of a doctor from Kenya. She also became good friends with Grace Lee, her Korean-Canadian roommate, and a Mexican girl named Blanca. We were happy that Heather had friends from all different countries and backgrounds.

Best of all, each year Heather spent at CID, she made two years of academic progress. The test results confirmed what anyone could tell just from listening to her conversation. CID had really worked. Heather had made remarkable progress in her speech.

Heather could only spend three years at CID because the school didn't take students older than fourteen. CID wanted to prepare their students for a regular school setting, and that job had to be done by the end of junior high school. Any longer was probably too late.

In the spring of 1987, the CID school officials indicated that Heather was doing so well that she would be able to go to a regular high school that fall. I was thrilled. Heather would even be with the same class of kids she had started kindergarten with eight years before! For me it was a dream come true.

Heather enjoyed her last year in St. Louis as much as she had her first. But she also was looking forward to coming home that summer for good.

I remember one warm spring evening she called me long distance to tell me she could hardly wait for the school year to end. "It will be so wonderful!" she exclaimed. "I will be home next year, and we will all be a family again!"

I didn't have the heart to tell her that might not be possible.

7

High School Years

What Heather didn't know was that her father and I had been having serious marital problems for some time. And although we hadn't yet done anything official, just days earlier we had decided it was time to consider a legal separation.

There were several reasons Heather didn't know. Our problems got worse once Heather left home and went to CID. She hadn't been home very much during those three years. When Heather was home, because we wanted that time to be special for her, both her father and I worked hard to keep most of our problems hidden. Besides, Heather could not hear us argue, and she could not hear the emotion behind the words she did hear. Heather simply didn't realize what would have been obvious if she'd not been deaf.

After that phone call, we decided for Heather's sake to give our marriage another try. But so many things had changed that, despite our best efforts, Heather wasn't really coming home to the same family she had left.

Her sisters had grown as much as she had. Melissa, who'd always been Heather's best friend, was now a popular student and track star with her own interests and a new set of friends. Stacey was graduating from high school that spring with plans to leave for college later that summer. So we all knew things would be different for our family.

I worried about Heather's upcoming freshman year. At CID Heather had been in small classes with other deaf children. In contrast, Dothan's Northview High School was one of the largest high school campuses in Alabama at the time with more than 2,500 students.

But I was amazed at how well prepared Heather was to cope in a regular high school. The study skills CID had taught her served Heather well. So while she worked very hard and spent long hours every night to keep up with her class work, she began pulling A's and B's from the very beginning of her high school career.

*   *   *

Heather had tried to keep up her dancing while she was at CID, even though she could not take lessons there. In the summer, she took lessons back home at Dothan. But when Heather moved back to Dothan and began year-round dance lessons again, I began to realize how committed she was to ballet. When she said she wanted to be a professional ballet dancer, I knew she was serious. I also knew that no matter how much talent Heather had, how much she loved to dance, and how committed she was, becoming a professional ballet dancer would not be an easy dream to achieve—even if she hadn't been deaf.

Then one day we heard about the Alabama School of Fine Arts, a public high school up in Birmingham with a special emphasis on the performing arts. It had strict entrance requirements and talent qualifications. Heather was interested, so she sent for information, and we went for a visit.

Though ASFA had never had any deaf students, everyone treated Heather with consideration and respect. However, the director of the school, Dr. Nelson, was very straightforward. "You know, Heather, of all the fine arts careers, professional ballet may be the hardest to break into," he told her.

His words didn't faze Heather a bit. "I love ballet," she said. "I realize that it will require a lot of work. But I'm used to working hard. And I want to be a ballet dancer."

I think Dr. Nelson was impressed by Heather's determination. He arranged a special tryout, and Heather was accepted for the next school year.

In the meantime, Heather's father moved out, and we were soon divorced. So that summer Melissa and I decided to go to Birmingham with Heather. I got a new teaching job there, and we all moved in with Granddad and Grandmother Gray until we could sell our house in Dothan.

Since Heather's aunt Stephanie and cousin Trey already lived there, Heather, Melissa, and I shared a bedroom and a single closet. At bedtime, I think my poor girls must have felt as though we were on that old television series *The Waltons*. "Good night, Grand-dad! Good night, Grandma. Night, Mom. Good night, Aunt Steph. Sleep tight, Trey. Don't let the bedbugs bite. Good night, Melissa. Night, Heather."

Being crowded wasn't the most difficult problem we faced. An even bigger daily challenge was Heather's schoolwork. ASFA had never had a deaf student before. The teachers tried to be helpful, but they didn't know how to help a hearing impaired student.

Heather enjoyed the opportunity to train for three hours and more every day under her respected dance instructor, Sonja Arova. In addition to the daily ninety-minute ballet class, Sonja required an additional workout every day after school. Heather seemed to greatly enjoy her daily workout routine, even though it was physically exhausting.

But things didn't go so well in other classes. The biggest problem was with the audio-trainer Heather had to use in every class. All her teachers gladly wore the mike/transmitter portion of the device. But when Heather turned on her receiver, her teachers' voices were often interrupted by nearby truckers talking on their CBs. "Breaker, breaker," they'd say. "Ten-four, good buddy!" No matter what frequency we tried, trucker talk would drown out most of Heather's teachers. That made classroom learning nearly impossible.

We began to tape all of Heather's classes. As soon as we got home each evening, Heather would work on her algebra assignment, and I would transcribe that day's tapes for all her other subjects. As soon as I'd finish one tape, I'd pass my handwritten notes to Heather. Then she could begin reading the lecture while I went on to the tape of the next class. A lot of nights Aunt Stephanie, Grandmother, or both would help with the transcribing. Still, it was usually ten or eleven o'clock before we finished providing Heather with the information she needed to complete her homework and feel prepared for the next day's classes.

For Heather, it was like completing two days' worth of work every day. The effort paid off with consistent A's and B's on her report card. But combined with her grueling dance schedule, her academic success took its toll on Heather, emotionally and physically. It took its toll on me as well. In fact, I don't think either of us would have survived that year without the support of my family.

That spring, when Heather brought home the registration forms for the next year's class schedule, I said, "You know, Heather, you've had a tough year here at ASFA. I think it's been good for you, especially for your dance. And you've made terrific grades. But I don't know if we as a family can go through another year like this one."

"I know," Heather replied. "And I realize my education is more important than my dancing."

We talked for a while about the options. "Some of the girls get too caught up in dancing," she told me. "They are too competitive. I don't want to be that way."

Heather told me she would be happy to transfer to Berry High School, where Melissa went. In fact, she said she would look forward to going to a regular high school again. And I assured her that we would somehow, somewhere, find a way for her to continue to develop her dance. Even though I didn't know how.

8

The Choice

We couldn't afford to pay for Heather to take dance *and* speech therapy, so we opted for dance. We found a Christian dance troupe in Birmingham called the Briarwood Ballet; Heather absolutely loved the daily workouts and frequent performances. Before long she gained a whole new vision of how she could use her dance to worship God.

Heather also enjoyed Berry High, even though it was her third high school in three years. But it helped that Melissa had gone there the year before. And Heather knew a lot of Berry students from the youth group at church. So she adjusted very well.

Fortunately, the academic situation was much better for Heather at Berry. Heather earned her usual A's and B's but without the amount of blood, sweat, and tears we'd invested the year before at ASFA.

That junior year we also visited Jacksonville State University, where Heather planned to attend after she graduated from high school. Not only were the folks at JSU committed to helping their hearing impaired students succeed, they answered all our questions honestly.

Dan Miller, the director of JSU's deaf-education support program, was the one who said Heather needed to learn how to communicate in sign. "All our interpreters have to use sign because that's the only universal way for them to interact with all the students. If Heather can't understand what's being communicated to other deaf students, she's going to miss out on one of the primary resources we provide for our hearing impaired students."

On the ninety-minute drive home from Jacksonville State, Heather said, "I think he is right, Mother. I need to learn sign."

I finally had to agree. "If you want to learn sign, I guess maybe it's time," I told her.

Part of my ongoing argument against sign had been that Heather could always learn it later. But first I wanted her to learn how to speak well. I'd always known that Heather would want to learn sign someday. Once she knew both oral language and sign, Heather could be a part of both worlds—the hearing world all of us live in *and* the smaller deaf world with its own rich and unique culture.

When Heather's advisor learned Heather wanted to learn sign, she talked to the high school administration and got permission to organize and teach a course in Signing Exact English (SEE) that next semester for any interested Berry High students. While Heather was the only deaf person in the class, more than a dozen hearing students signed up and took the course with her.

One of those, a bright and popular girl by the name of Misha Jones, became Heather's closest and dearest high school friend. Sign language helped to forge their friendship. They had a "secret language" that enabled them to have private talks, because no one could "overhear" them! They could even "talk" during class without being caught by their teachers.

Like most teenagers, Heather wanted to fit in with the crowd. Usually she wore her hair in a style that covered her hearing aid. As a result, many of her high school classmates never realized she was deaf.

I remember the afternoon she picked me up after school and told me about an acquaintance who'd asked her, "Are you too big a snob to speak when I say 'hi' to you in the hall?"

"I just did not hear her," Heather complained to

me. "Now she thinks I am a snob. I feel awful about that. Do you think there are other people who think that?"

"There might be," I told her. "But the only way to avoid that is to be open about your hearing. Tell people you meet that you are deaf. Remind friends to speak directly to you when you are looking."

Lunchtime was especially miserable for Heather. She found it nearly impossible to pick voices out of the constant roar of cafeteria commotion in her ear. That meant she had to rely almost totally on lipreading. "I get tired of asking my friends to repeat what I don't hear," she admitted. "And I think sometimes they get tired of me asking. So I just laugh when the people around me laugh. That makes me sad. I just want to be part of the conversation. But I'm not."

*   *   *

Between her junior and senior years of high school, Heather went to Jackson, Mississippi, for a summer workshop conducted by a touring Christian dance company called the Ballet Magnificat. Again she learned that dance could be a beautiful and powerful way to witness for and worship God.

"I think God is calling me to be a dancer," she announced when she got home.

"That may be, Heather," I told her. "But I'm sure he also wants you to get an education. Professional dancers can't dance forever. You need to be thinking about other possible careers. And a good place to start is to consider your strengths. What subjects have you always enjoyed and done best in?"

"Math," she replied.

"Then accounting might be a very good option for you," I told her. "I know a number of CPAs who make a very comfortable living. You could do that full-time or maybe part-time for a while and still keep up with your dancing on the side."

Heather thought that made a lot of sense. She even took a course in accounting her senior year to see how she would like it.

Whenever Heather thought or talked about college, the subject of money usually came up. Heather knew enough about our financial situation to understand it wouldn't be easy.

"Lots of college kids work to help pay their expenses," she said. "I could get a part-time job."

But Heather's hearing impairment had always made her education a full-time job in itself. College, we knew, would be even more difficult than high school. Heather wouldn't have time for a job.

Then we stumbled upon another solution. The fall of her senior year of high school, someone suggested that Heather should compete in the Shelby County Junior Miss Pageant. Their prizes included scholarship money that would help pay her way in college.

I read the pageant's statement of purpose and goals. The booklet said they were looking for young women with poise, leadership ability, talent, and a number of other valuable character traits. Heather qualified on all those points.

I helped Heather fill out all the pageant application forms. Then the two of us began learning just how much was involved in preparing for a pageant. So many plans, so little time.

I took the sleeves out of the green bridesmaid dress Heather had worn three years before in Stacey's wedding, added some rhinestones, and made a few other alterations to transform it into an evening gown.

For Heather's talent, we adapted one of her Briarwood costumes. Then we spent hours editing down Twila Paris' Christian inspirational hit "How Beautiful!" to the required length for the talent segment of the pageant. In addition to practicing her own talent, Heather had long, nightly rehearsals with all the girls in the competition for a full two weeks prior to the November competition.

While the dance requirements of the rehearsals seemed rather simple and fun to Heather, those girls without a dance background sometimes had trouble with it. One contestant in particular, whose talent was singing, struggled with even the basic dance steps. "I just can't do it," she complained after she'd messed up the routine for the umpteenth time. But when the director called the next break, Heather hurried over to the frustrated girl.

"Come on," Heather told her. "I'm going to help you do this. I know you can. Here, watch me. Like this . . ." And every chance she could after that, Heather encouraged and worked with her new friend until the girl began to catch on.

Like many large pageant competitions, Shelby County Junior Miss was a three-night affair. One-half of the contestants performs talent while the other half models evening gowns on each of the two preliminary nights. At that point, the judges narrow the field to ten finalists who are announced soon after all the contestants are introduced on the final evening. Then, in the course of that last night's program, each finalist performs her talent, models her evening gown, and answers an impromptu question onstage as a measure of poise.

Heather took first place in the talent competition and won the spirit award as the person all the girls voted as the most encouraging, friendly, and cooperative. Once all the other scholarships had been announced, it was finally time to announce the winner. *Could it be?*

"Second runner-up, Miss Heather Whitestone!"

So she didn't win. But her entire family, even her father Bill, proudly hugged and congratulated her. Heather was absolutely thrilled to total up her winnings

and realize she was taking home $1,400 in scholar-
ships to apply toward next year's college expenses.
That was more than she might have made from any
part-time job flipping burgers after school.

*   *   *

Not that everything was perfect Heather's senior
year. There were still times at school when her hearing
impairment made her feel as if she didn't belong. Sometimes she wondered if she would have been better off if
she had gone to deaf schools—where she would have
grown up with other kids who shared her handicap and
understood her frustrations.

Those feelings were a big part of the reason
Heather decided to enter the Miss Deaf Alabama competition the summer after she graduated from high
school. "This weekend will be good for you, Mother,"
she said. "You will see what it's really like in the deaf
world. You will be the one who doesn't belong."

The Miss Deaf Alabama competition was held on
the campus of the Alabama School for the Deaf in
Talladega. Once we'd found the dorm and checked
into our room, I took a walk while Heather went to
a meeting of pageant contestants. When she finally
returned to the room, I could tell something was
bothering her.

"What happened?" I wanted to know.

She told me she had met the other girls who

would be in the pageant—just six of them. They'd made fun of her for bringing her mother along. Heather said they seemed even more irritated to learn I was a "hearing" mother. They angrily told Heather it was time she grew up and left her "hearing family." They said she didn't need us. And they insisted that the deaf community was her "only real family."

I wanted to march out, find those girls, and give them a piece of my mind. But I bit my tongue.

"They told me I absolutely should not talk onstage," Heather went on. "They told me only sign!"

That command didn't sit well with Heather. Before she left the room for the pageant the next evening she told me, "I don't care what they say. I am going to speak!"

That may have been part of the reason Heather didn't win. That and the fact that the mostly deaf audience couldn't hear the music of Heather's ballet at all, so they merely saw a girl flitting and spinning and jumping around the stage. They weren't at all impressed. Heather finished her wonderful routine to only a smattering of polite applause.

I knew it wasn't going to be Heather's night even before the winners were announced. But it did seem a little surprising that she didn't even get one of the three runner-up spots.

Heather was so discouraged by that experience that she didn't feel like talking on the long drive home.

In fact, Heather moped around—crying and angry—
for two days after we got back. To hear her talk, her
life was ruined because she didn't belong in either the
hearing *or* the deaf world.

As bad as I felt for the tough time Heather had at
the Miss Deaf Alabama Pageant, I quickly tired of that
attitude. Finally I walked into her room on that second
day and said, "You and I need to talk."

I said I was truly sorry her feelings had been hurt,
but I also told her, "It seems to me you've come to one
of life's crossroads. It's time for you to decide which
world you plan to live in—the hearing world or the
deaf world.

"If you decide you want to live in the hearing
world, you can go to JSU like you planned this fall. If
you're convinced your future lies in the deaf world,
maybe you want to consider going to Washington,
D.C. and checking out Galludet [the country's leading
deaf college]. But that decision is up to you now. I
won't make it for you.

"But I have to tell you that after this weekend, I
am absolutely convinced once and for all that the
choices I made for you were the right choices. I am
glad that we didn't put you in the deaf world, especially
if they believe that your hearing family shouldn't be a
part of their world. I wanted more than anything else
for you to be a part of my world and for me to always
be a part of yours.

"You're an adult now. I can't tell you what to do anymore. But I'll always be your mother. And I'll always love you.

"What you choose to do now is totally and completely up to you."

That was when Heather cried and told me how the other girls at the Miss Deaf Alabama Pageant had shunned her and given her a difficult time. That's also when she told me about the post-pageant trip to Pizza Hut and how none of the other girls could make the waiter, who didn't know sign language, understand what they wanted to order. Finally Heather, who did understand enough sign to know what the others wanted, ordered orally for everyone at the table.

"It would have been so much easier if they had just known how to speak," she concluded. "I see it is an advantage if deaf people can speak. Then you can communicate in both worlds."

"That's what I've always thought," I said.

"I've been thinking," Heather added. "Maybe God wants me to be a bridge between the two worlds. Like I was in that Pizza Hut between the waiter and those other girls."

I thought that was a wonderful dream. "How do you want to do that?" I asked. "Are you ready to start at JSU like you planned? Or do you want to start in the deaf world and maybe go to Galludet?"

Without hesitation Heather replied, "I want to go to JSU."

The decision was made. Whether she would become an accountant, a professional dancer, or maybe something else entirely, remained to be seen. But from that day on we both knew one thing for sure: Heather wanted to be a bridge between the hearing and deaf worlds.

And we had to believe that dream would come true someday.

9

Miss JSU

By the time she started college at JSU the fall of 1991, Heather had begun to do a lot of serious thinking about her future and her goals. In a writing assignment for one of her classes, Heather began a short essay entitled "My Life Goal" with this opening statement: "What I want most to accomplish in my life is to become Miss America."

In her essay Heather went on to describe how she had watched her first Miss America Pageant on TV when she was seven. She had been thrilled to see one of the contestants dance a ballet routine, and for years as she practiced her own dance she would imagine performing in Atlantic City herself one day. Winning the talent in the Shelby County Junior Miss Pageant the year before had rekindled her dream of becoming Miss America. As Miss America, she concluded, she could witness for God and be an encouragement to others, "especially the little deaf children."

The first pieces of the foundation upon which Heather would build that dream were already being laid. One early fall day Heather met Teresa Strickland, a former Miss Alabama who worked at JSU. "I was in a beauty pageant last year," Heather told Teresa. "But I only came in second runner-up. Would you like to see my pictures sometime?"

"Sure," Teresa told her. "Bring your photos to my office. I'd love to see them."

Within the week Heather returned to the admissions office to show Teresa her photographs from the Shelby County Junior Miss Pageant. When Teresa spotted the picture of Heather doing her talent routine, it raised her curiosity. "You dance ballet, Heather? That's great. But tell me, how do you hear the music?" After Heather explained that we had started her in ballet as listening therapy and how she'd gone on to dance at ASFA and with the Briarwood Ballet, Teresa was obviously impressed. "So many girls in pageants today are singers," she told Heather. "With your ballet, maybe you ought to think about entering the Miss Jacksonville State Pageant."

The two of them talked a while longer. Heather asked a lot of questions and learned that not only had Teresa been Miss Alabama, but she'd gone on to be named first runner-up in the Miss America competition. "Did you win a lot of scholarship money?" Heather wanted to know.

Teresa explained that her scholarship money had paid all her graduate school expenses. "If you're interested in scholarship money, Heather, that's a good reason to go out for 'Miss JSU.' The winner gets a full year's tuition. And the prize for talent is a free semester."

That really got Heather's attention. She told Teresa she'd certainly think about it.

When Heather told me she wanted to enter the Miss Jacksonville State Pageant I was pleased. And when she told me that she would also like to enter the Miss St. Clair competition (another local pageant scheduled only two weeks prior to Miss JSU) for the added experience, I agreed that a little practice never hurts. But neither of us knew yet what would be involved: lots of time, even more money, and loads of paperwork.

Heather could wear the same costume for the talent routine she'd worked up for the Junior Miss Pageant the year before. But she needed a new evening gown and other clothes to wear for the interviews with the judges. The Miss Alabama/Miss America pageant system requires each contestant to have her own individual platform—some significant social issue of the day that she is able to speak out on, and a practical plan for implementing that program. So Heather had a complete personal platform to pull together on top of all the other preparations.

With Stacey, Heather, and me all working together, we had Heather primed and ready to go for the Miss St. Clair Pageant on February 29, 1992. That was a night none of us will ever forget.

Heather looked great during the swimsuit and evening gown portions of the competition that evening. She danced well, too. The trouble came with the impromptu questions onstage.

"Heather," she was asked, "as someone who obviously knows and loves ballet, tell us, who is your favorite dancer? And why?"

I winced because I knew the "who" she was going to say. I could only pray she'd be able to pronounce his name clearly enough for the judges.

Heather turned toward the audience and smiled. "My favorite dancer is Mikhail Baryshnikov." She spoke with such poise and the words came out so clearly, I wanted to cheer. I breathed a big sigh of relief as the question was repeated. "And why?"

Maybe Heather panicked at that point. Maybe her brain froze for a moment. We'll never know because Heather can't explain it herself. All she managed to say in response to the question about *why* she admired the great Russian dancer Mikhail Baryshnikov so much was: "He jumps high!"

That was all she said; she made no attempt at recovery. *He jumps high?* That sounded like something she might have said in the third grade.

Heather didn't win anything that night. When the large crowd of family and friends hurried up to greet her after the program, she acted embarrassed.

As the audience quickly filed out of the auditorium and I waited in front of the stage for Heather to get dressed, Teresa Strickland sought me out, pulled me aside, and said, "Please don't let Heather give up on pageants, even though I have a feeling she might want to after tonight." She went on to tell me how moved she'd been by Heather's dance. "I see tremendous potential in Heather," Teresa concluded. "She'll do better in the Miss JSU Pageant."

"I'm not going to be in the Miss JSU Pageant!" Heather declared when I told her what Teresa had said. "I am never going to enter another pageant. I was so embarrassed!" Heather complained. "It was awful! I was terrible!"

I stopped her at that point and finally got her to admit that she'd done fine in the swimsuit, evening gown, and talent portions of the pageant. "The only problem was the interview question," I assured her.

"You might want to practice a little more for that. But everything else was fine."

Heather finally did change her mind. Twenty-three girls entered the one-night pageant for Miss Jacksonville State University. Once again Heather made a fine appearance in the swimsuit and evening gown portions of the program. And as the long night wore on, I decided she had a great chance to win talent. I knew that would make her feel a lot better. I only hoped that she would make it through the question portion without being embarrassed again.

When the long-dreaded question time finally came, Heather stepped confidently to the mike. "Heather, do you think it's right for our U.S. congressmen and senators to be able to vote themselves pay raises? Tell us why or why not."

Oh, man! I thought. *What I wouldn't give for that question about Mikhail Baryshnikov!*

But Heather nailed it this time. I was so nervous I don't remember exactly what she said, but she didn't hesitate at all. Whatever she said sounded logical and clear. *She made it through!*

Finally the program wound to a close. All twenty-three girls lined up for the announcement of winners. The first contestant called was fourth runner-up. Then the emcee realized she should have started with the talent winner and backtracked, saying, "The winner of the talent portion of tonight's competition and the recipient of one semester's tuition to Jacksonville State University, Miss Heather Whitestone."

I knew from the confused look on Heather's face she didn't know what she'd won. Perhaps she figured they'd named her third runner-up. I knew she'd be thrilled with the semester scholarship as soon as we explained it all to her afterwards.

The rest of the announcements followed in order. Third runner-up. Second runner-up. First runner-up. And then "Miss Jacksonville State University for 1992 ... Miss Heather Whitestone!"

Suddenly our family and friends were all shouting and cheering. I was absolutely and totally shocked Heather had won—not because she is deaf, but because she was just a freshman. I didn't know if there'd ever been a freshman selected as Miss JSU.

Winning Miss JSU automatically qualified Heather for that year's Miss Alabama Pageant. Miss Alabama required more preparation than any other pageant Heather had entered before. There seemed to be some kind of deadline every week from the end of March until the middle of May. We needed two edited copies of Heather's "How Beautiful" music on reel-to-reel tapes. She needed a portfolio of professional photos. They wanted a more complete and refined treatment of her platform. The list of things we had to do, prepare, and plan seemed endless.

For the most part, Heather and I got along well

during all the hours of planning and preparation. But on one issue Heather and I had a very real difference of opinion—her hairstyle.

Heather preferred it down because it was simpler; I argued that it made her look far too young. I thought she looked so much older and more sophisticated with it up; she thought it a pain to fix and keep her hair on top of her head. We'd gone round and round on the subject until the afternoon of the last day before I was to deliver her to the pageant officials on the Samford University campus in Birmingham.

Because every contestant in the Miss Alabama Pageant is required to fix her own hair, Heather was sitting in front of the mirror in her bedroom, fretting and fussing. Her dark hair is so fine that no matter how she pinned it, large strands kept slipping out of place.

Frustrated with her hair and irritated with me for preferring it up, Heather finally declared, "I am not wearing it up, Mother! I can't get it to stay!"

"You can't wear it down," I told her.

"It's my hair!"

"Just take that banana clip with you. You need to wear it up!"

"I like it better down!"

I think we were both ready to scream when Aunt Stephanie stopped by. "Could you please go see if you can help Heather figure out what to do with her hair?" I pleaded.

It took a while. But with my staying out of the way, the two of them finally came up with a style that Heather thought she could manage by herself. I wanted to shout hallelujahs and hug my little sister for her help. But I didn't say a word, for fear it would change Heather's mind again.

Heather's aunt Stephanie had actually come by that day not just to say good-bye and wish Heather good luck, but also to help me finish up some little surprises she and I had planned. During a pre-pageant workshop for mothers, one of the women had suggested that we send a special little creative gift or note of encouragement for our daughters to open each day of the week that they spent preparing for the pageant.

The surprise Stephanie and I had cooked up for Heather's first day at the pageant was our biggest. Someone had advised Heather early on that she might practice her interview by placing stuffed animals in chairs around a room and talking to them like pretend judges. She'd been doing that for weeks and had actually packed a couple small animals to take with her for extra practice that final week. But Stephanie and I knew she'd be too embarrassed to show up at Miss Alabama carrying her all-time favorite stuffed animal—her old, love-worn friend, Pooh Bear. So we packed Pooh Bear into a big box with a note saying, "After I've been with you all these years, I knew there was no way you were going to make it through this week without me. So I stowed away, and here I am!"

I could imagine her acting embarrassed and exclaiming, "Oh, Mother!" when she opened the package Stephanie and I had wrapped. But I also knew she'd be pleased to have Pooh Bear with her.

Once I dropped Heather off at Samford University Monday morning, I hardly saw her again all week except onstage. The pageant officials kept the girls hidden away on campus for an intensive week of rehearsing, interviewing, and preparation for the four nights of competition.

* * *

The last evening of the Miss Alabama Pageant began with Heather among the finalists. That meant she went through every part of the program again that night onstage. The crowd warmed to Heather from the start. She got a long applause when she came out in her blue sequined evening gown and made her twenty-second platform summary statement: "With positive self-esteem, courage, inner strength, and God's help, the impossible is indeed possible."

By the time she finished dancing to "How Beautiful" she had the entire audience entranced. *Maybe, just maybe, she's got a shot at winning!*

When they announced that Heather was the overall talent winner, I felt even better about her chances.

So when she got first runner-up, I couldn't help feeling a little disappointed knowing she'd come so, so close.

Heather herself was absolutely elated. She'd already decided she would go for the title again the following year.

The very next morning Heather awakened complaining of terrible pain in her jaws. Early Monday morning, less than thirty-six hours after the Miss Alabama Pageant ended, I made an emergency dental appointment for Heather to have four impacted wisdom teeth removed. That same afternoon Heather, unable to talk herself, insisted I call the officials of the Miss Point Mallard Pageant in Decatur, one of the first qualifying competitions in the state for the next year's Miss Alabama Pageant. She planned to compete there on the Fourth of July weekend—now barely a week and a half away.

I made the call. But as I looked at my daughter's swollen face and shook my head, I said, "Too bad there's not a Miss Chipmunk Pageant starting somewhere tomorrow. You couldn't lose."

At least she didn't hurt too much to laugh.

10

First Runner-Up

Heather's competition for Miss Point Mallard included a half dozen or more very familiar faces— girls she'd competed against in the state pageant in Birmingham just two weekends before. These girls, like Heather, had already decided to pursue their dreams another year. They were anxious to get the first step in next year's Miss Alabama qualifying process out of the way.

Because this was Heather's fourth pageant in less than five months, our family felt like true pageant veterans. While we warned Heather and each other not to be overconfident, I was not surprised when they crowned Heather "Miss Point Mallard 1992."

Evidently I wasn't the only one to anticipate that result. The mother of one of the other girls walked up to congratulate me that evening saying, "Good for Heather! Now that she's won this title, the rest of the girls will have their chance." In her mind at least, Heather was an early favorite to become the next Miss Alabama.

I hoped she was right. But doubts were raised when I learned that not everyone felt as charitable toward my daughter.

Later that summer I received an unexpected long-distance call from one of my closest friends from Dothan. She had just learned that a mutual friend of ours had overheard a pageant insider tell a Dothan business owner, "There will never be a deaf girl chosen as Miss Alabama! Heather Whitestone doesn't stand a chance next year!"

I never did mention the incident to Heather because I knew it would only upset her. I was thankful that I didn't need to worry about her finding out on her own. One of the few advantages to Heather's handicap is that her deafness filters out most rumors and gossip. I figured what she didn't know, and wouldn't know, couldn't hurt her.

* * *

Heather and I both agreed that if she hoped to

become Miss America, her dance routine could stand to have a little more excitement and emotion in it. So for weeks I went from one store to another in search of another contemporary Christian song that would fulfill all our requirements. Not only did we need a beautiful song with appropriate lyrics and dramatic changes of pace and mood, but it had to be sung by a singer whose voice Heather could hear. And we had to be able to cut it down to the exact length allowed for each talent portion of the competition—two minutes and forty-five seconds.

By late summer, we'd made no progress. Then Heather and I attended a Miss Alabama Musical Revue where Kim Wimmer, the girl who had beaten Heather out for Miss Alabama 1992, sang her own version of the Sandi Patty hit "Via Dolorosa," a song about Christ's crucifixion. As Kim sang that gorgeous number, I suddenly knew. God had given me the answer. In my mind I could already envision Heather dancing to "Via Dolorosa."

At first Heather didn't want to use the song because Kim often sang it. But I kept playing and replaying the song for Heather. She loved the music and the lyrics. And when we couldn't find anything else she liked nearly as well, she finally agreed to use "Via Dolorosa" after all. She and her new dance instructor, Monica Barnett Smith, began choreographing the movements early that fall. They perfected the routine for months. Fall, winter, and spring Heather worked on it almost every day.

In March we suddenly realized we might have a serious problem. It dawned on us that if one of the other contestants applied first and wanted to sing "Via Dolorosa" (we knew one local pageant winner had used it for her vocal talent), Heather would be forced to choose another number. We'd already choreo-graphed and costumed the song. If we couldn't use it, months of hard work and hundreds of hours of prac-tice would go down the drain.

We decided we had only one hope. Heather would have to file her application first. And since application packets for all contestants went out at the same time— after the last local pageant every spring—we figured out what we had to do to manage it.

The minute Heather's package was delivered to the Point Mallard Pageant Director in Decatur, Beverly Walker called Heather's grandparents with the mes-sage (I was at school). Beverly filled out all the forms required from her before she drove to meet Granddad Gray and me late that night at a rest stop halfway between Decatur and Birmingham. There the two of us spread out the papers on a formica countertop, and Beverly went over everything Heather and I needed to do to complete all the remaining forms.

I stayed up most of the night typing in everything I could do by myself, and the next day after school I

drove to Jacksonville with the packet to get Heather's
input and signature. At home again that night I typed
up everything Heather had given me. And the next day
I took personal leave from school so I could get everything notarized and delivered in person to the Miss
Alabama office in downtown Birmingham.

"Hi, Daphne." Sandra Gardner, the secretary and
only paid employee for Miss Alabama, knew me well.
"You've got Heather's application forms? Great. You're
just the second one to file."

"Second?" I felt a sudden panic.

"The first one came in just a few minutes ago."

"Who was it?"

When she told me I felt my heart sink clear to my
shoes. It was the one girl we'd been most worried
about—the very one who'd sung "Via Dolorosa" to win
her local qualifying pageant.

My heart sank.

"Well, Daphne," Sandra Gardner said as she paged
through the application forms, "let's make sure everything is in order here before you go."

"Oh." She paused. "Heather's decided to change
the music for her talent routine! She wants to use 'Via
Dolorosa'?"

Oh, boy! I thought. *Here it comes now!*

"That will be a beautiful number for Heather's
dance. Tell her good luck; everything looks in order
here."

The other girl must have changed her mind. She was singing a different number for her talent in the state pageant.

Thank you, Lord!

*   *   *

Pageant week finally arrived. It turns out, I learned later, that Heather felt her pre-competition interview didn't go very well. One of the judges looked down at her notes while she asked her question and another had a long mustache; Heather had difficulty understanding them. But what had upset Heather most was her own answer to a question she thought she did understand.

One of the judges asked, "How many people are there in your family, Heather?"

"Oh . . ." she hesitated. "I don't know exactly. Thirty. Maybe forty."

"I was so embarrassed!" Heather told me later. "I did not realize at first that he was asking about brothers or sisters. I was including my grandparents, aunts, uncles, and all my cousins."

"I don't think you have any reason to feel embarrassed," I told her. "In fact, I think you answered that question the way God intended it to be answered, because he's given you a very big family of people who care about you."

But that chance for reassurance didn't come until

later. During pageant week itself I could only wonder what was happening and watch Heather onstage during the preliminaries every night. And of course I prayed for Heather and hoped the little one-a-day gifts Aunt Stephanie and I had sent along again this year would help bolster her spirits.

I liked the figure of Sebastian Crab (from Disney's *The Little Mermaid*) that we sent on the day of her swimsuit competition and the note that reminded Heather (who was never a morning person): "Don't be crabby today." But my favorite gift, because I knew it would make Heather laugh, was one of those ugly little plastic troll figures with the wild red hair. I'd carefully rolled the doll's bright red tresses into a tiny bun on top of its head and attached a little sign that said: "Troll Hair Patrol: Wear it up!"

We had a bigger entourage of friends and family than ever before that year. They all came all four nights. And we weren't the only ones who thought Heather would win.

The grapevine was buzzing all week. Saturday morning at home I received a phone call from a good friend who had volunteered to work during the pageant. She'd overheard backstage talk that some insiders were saying Heather Whitestone could not win because she was deaf. "I'm not calling to upset you," she said, "but I wanted you to be prepared because I know a lot of people consider Heather the favorite."

"It's okay. It's in the Lord's hands now," I told her.

To tell the truth, I was seething inside. That night, when Heather was named first runner-up again, I felt very frustrated and angry with the whole pageant system.

I knew Heather well enough to tell how terribly disappointed she was. But she didn't break down and cry until she was back with her family and friends.

"I thought you should have won," I told her. "But since you didn't, we will just have to believe it wasn't God's timing. If you want to try again next year, I'm with you. If you don't, fine. Either way," I assured her, "it will be your decision."

Heather went backstage to gather her things, and our friends Jim and Vicky Davis walked up. "Do you think she'll go again?" Vicky asked. "She shouldn't give up!"

"To tell you the truth, Vicky, I don't know," I replied. "I'll certainly back her if she decides to try next year. But I've never seen her this discouraged. So I don't have any idea what she will decide."

To help her make her decision, the Davises paid for Heather to attend the Miss America Pageant in Atlantic City that September. Her aunt Stephanie and I paid our own way to go with her.

A lot of encouraging things happened on that trip. By Saturday morning of pageant week in Atlantic City, after three nights of preliminaries and the big, traditional

Friday night Miss America parade, everyone in the Alabama delegation agreed that Kalyn Chapman, Miss Alabama, had earned a spot among the ten semifinalists and maybe even had a shot at the crown.

But the possibility that Kalyn would become Miss America really made Heather feel torn. Part of her was rooting for her friend. But I knew that wasn't the way she wanted to become Miss Alabama! As first runner-up to Miss Alabama, Heather would be required to take over Kalyn's duties for the coming year if Kalyn were crowned Miss America. And that would make Heather, as reigning Miss Alabama, ineligible for the next year's state and national pageants.

"We've said all along that we had to trust the Lord and his timing," I told her.

"I know," Heather said. "But it really bothers me to feel this way. Do you think you and Aunt Stephanie could pray with me about it just before we go to the pageant tonight? That whatever happens, the Lord will give me peace about it?"

"Okay," we agreed. And we did.

Kalyn Chapman did make the semifinals that night. But she wasn't named as one of the five finalists. Kimberly Aiken of Columbia, South Carolina, was crowned Miss America 1994.

Membership in the official Miss Alabama delegation gave us backstage privileges. So when most of the crowd filed out the back of the auditorium, we headed upstairs to a ballroom jammed with friends and fans anxiously awaiting their first post-pageant look at the new Miss America. It was after midnight before Kim finally arrived for a brief appearance and victory speech.

When we'd finally wormed our way out of the ballroom, Heather asked if we could go back down to the convention hall for "one more look." Stephanie and I nodded and tagged along.

The cameras and the crowd were all gone. The massive hall was empty by this time, except for a small crew of workmen dismantling the sets and readying the stage for the next big event.

"Do you think they'd let me walk out on the runway?" Heather wondered.

"You'll never know unless you ask," I said.

So she walked up the stage steps and over to one of the crew. "Is it okay if I walk out on the runway?" she asked.

The guy looked up, nodding. "Sure, why not?"

"Is it okay if my mother goes with me?"

The workman give a shrug. "What do I care?"

Heather motioned for me to join her. As I made my way up onto the stage and looked down that famous runway my first thought was, "It's slick as glass. I hope I don't fall!"

But then Heather took my arm and we walked together down that long shiny runway in that empty convention center. First we waved down at Stephanie who was giving us a standing ovation. Then we began waving out at thousands of empty seats as if they were full of screaming, adoring fans.

I'm sure those workmen onstage, if they noticed us at all, must have been thinking, *Those people really need to get a life.*

But afterwards Heather told me it was at that moment, walking down the runway in that darkened Atlantic City Convention Center, that she finally made up her mind. *I'll give it one more chance. I'm going to do whatever it takes to come back here as a contestant in the Miss America Pageant next year.*

11

A Dream Come True

When we came home from Atlantic City and Heather said she'd made up her mind to enter Miss Alabama again, we checked out the list of upcoming local pageants. Heather decided to enter the Miss Cullman Area contest. Dancing again to "Via Dolorosa," Heather took the top talent award for her fifth straight pageant. And when the winner was announced, Heather was crowned Miss Cullman Area and had qualified once again for the Miss Alabama Pageant the following summer.

This year Heather said she thought she'd rather

concentrate her community service efforts on younger children. So she began to revamp her platform.

When Heather boiled her message down to five main points, we thought, *A star has five points!* And that's how we ended up with Heather's STARS program: Success Through Action and Realization of your dreamS. In her program for kids she emphasized one main point for each of the five points in a star:

1. Have a positive attitude.
2. Believe in your dreams.
3. Be willing to work very hard.
4. Be honest with yourself; face your weaknesses and obstacles.
5. Build a support team you can depend on.

These lessons all grew out of Heather's own life experience. She could deliver this advice with conviction and power because she'd seen it work.

We came up with a STARS booklet that Heather could hand out to older elementary students to remind them of her message. Then our friend Vicky Davis, who was principal of Green Valley Elementary, remembered that her school had a huge box of left-over plastic sheriff's stars. "If we spray paint those badges, Heather could use them as STARS pins— something to hand out to kindergartners or first graders who are too young to appreciate her booklet," Vicky suggested.

We all thought that was a great idea, so Heather went over to Vicky and Jim's one evening to paint those stars. The night grew so late that they were all getting tired and acting a little silly. Vicky held up a freshly painted gold star in front of each eye and said, "Glow, Heather, glow." They all laughed. But then they decided that might work somehow. After all, STARS shine, STARS glow.

That's how "Glow, Heather, glow!" became Heather's slogan. The students of Green Valley Elementary used the slogan on posters and banners throughout their school to welcome Heather, show their support for her Miss Alabama goal, and remind themselves of the STARS program's message. The Green Valley kids adopted Heather as part of a mutual support team that year (part of her point #5). And they responded so enthusiastically to Heather's message that she soon had offers to expand the program to other schools. Heather learned that she loved working with kids, and the kids certainly loved her.

Something else concerned us that year. The Davis's son-in-law Brandon approached us soon after Heather made her decision to pursue the Miss Alabama title a third year. "I don't know how you're going to take this," he said. "But I think there's one problem that has to be solved before Heather will ever be Miss Alabama. And that's the in-depth interview with the pageant judges."

He told us the problem wasn't the questions the judges asked. "The real hurdle for Heather is the one question they don't ask! Until Heather can answer that question to their satisfaction, I don't think she will ever win at the state or national level. And that question is this: Can a deaf girl handle the responsibilities of a Miss Alabama? Or a Miss America?

"I certainly believe Heather can. But she has to convince the judges first. To do that, she's first going to have to find a way to address that question no one wants to ask."

Fortunately solving that problem proved far simpler than we could ever have hoped. When we received the thick application packet from the state pageant office in April, we learned there had been a change in the judges' interview. On previous interviews, Heather had to walk into the room, state her name, and immediately begin fielding whatever questions the judges had for her. This year each contestant was given two minutes to make an opening statement before the formal questioning began.

Those two minutes would provide the chance Heather needed to address that crucial question none of the judges wanted to ask. But what exactly should Heather say?

*   *   *

Pageant week finally came again. We never said it

out loud, but Heather and I both knew that this was probably her last chance at winning Miss Alabama. And her last shot at her Miss America dream.

Early that week Heather had her interview with the judges. When she walked into the room, this is what she said:

"I am Heather Whitestone, Miss Cullman Area. When I was eighteen months old, I became very ill. The medicine given to me to save my life left me profoundly deaf. My mother was told that a normal life for me would be impossible, for example, that I'd never drive a car or go to a public school. But thank goodness the word *impossible* is not in my family's vocabulary. On Wednesday night you will see the results of believing in your dream. Now it's my turn to take all my resources and energies to bring about my dreams.

"I want to be Miss America, and I want to graduate from college. But I know each of you has a question in your mind, and I want to answer it for you right now: Can a profoundly deaf woman fulfill the duties of Miss Alabama and Miss America? To this I say, yes, I can do it! Because I realize that everything is possible with God's help. I don't see my deafness as an obstacle but as an opportunity for creative thinking. My STARS program has made it possible for me to go into elementary schools to express this message.

"I do want you to know that lipreading at its very

best will only give me about fifty percent of what you say. So I may repeat the question just to make sure I understand. Or I may ask you to write it down to save time.

"I'm excited about our interview. So let's begin."

*   *   *

Aunt Stephanie and I had sent our traditional one-a-day surprises for Heather to open that week. I knew she'd have the biggest surprise Thursday when she opened her gift to find that little troll with the red hair bun again. Heather had thrown the doll in the trash some months earlier. But I'd saved it with the thought of recycling it one more time for this year's state pageant. I sent it along with a little sign that said, "Just when you thought it was safe to let your hair down, the hair patrol is back. Keep it up!"

For Saturday, I'd wrapped a special little gift. I'd found a glass miniature of a coach and horses. With it I sent a note: "Like Cinderella, may all your dreams come true tonight, Heather. Love, Mom."

*   *   *

The third time was a charm. Heather finally won Miss Alabama.

And the week after that, she began a whirlwind schedule of appearances throughout the state. I could only imagine how thrilling all this must have been for

Heather. It was exciting for me just to see her picture in the papers or to hear about her on the radio. She kept so busy to start with I hardly got to talk with her on the phone.

I worried about Heather's health. I knew the summerlong demands of her Miss Alabama schedule had exhausted her. She'd been promised days off she never got. She sometimes made so many appearances in a day that she couldn't finish practicing her dance routine until ten or eleven at night.

I also worried as much, if not more, about her emotional well-being. How were her spirits? She could always put on a good front for strangers, and the people around her now were almost all strangers. They couldn't know how she really felt. How would she react when she had to go into the Miss America Pageant without her family support group? Who would be able to encourage her?

Heather's hearing impairment sheltered her from the conflict going on around her all summer. Looking back, I see how wonderfully God used Heather's personal strength of character and even her "weakness" to keep her focused. Although she did not have her family support system fully in place, Heather arrived in Atlantic City prepared to pursue her dream.

*   *   *

The Miss America contestants are divided into three groups. On Tuesday evening Heather and the rest of her group appeared in the evening gown segment of the preliminary program, while the other two groups competed in their swimsuit and talent divisions. Then the groups rotated. Since the results of the preliminary nights' evening gown competition is never publicly announced (it's held as a secret wild card in the judges' balloting), we had no official measure as to how she did that Tuesday night. Of course, Heather's large group of family and friends thought she was tops.

Then Wednesday evening Heather's fans went crazy when she won the swimsuit preliminary. None of us had expected that.

By Thursday morning the buzz up and down the boardwalk was about Heather: placing first in the swimsuit preliminary suddenly made her the girl to beat. The local newspapers were carrying human interest stories about the deaf contestant from Alabama. The *Atlantic Press* featured the pageant with cover-to-cover reports all week.

As much as we enjoyed the good press Heather received that week, we knew that what happened onstage was a lot more important. So of course we were all thrilled when Heather won her talent preliminary on Thursday night.

Being a double preliminary winner (swimsuit and talent) definitely put Heather in the running for the crown. However, some veteran pageant observers warned us that half the time it had happened, the double-preliminary winner had been named first runner-up on Saturday night.

I knew I'd be proud of Heather no matter what happened in the finals. So I told myself, *It doesn't matter.* But it did. Heather's dream had always been to become Miss America, not first runner-up. I couldn't imagine how disappointed she would be if she came so close to her dream and fell one step short.

*   *   *

By Saturday night there was such an incredible air of anticipation running through town, through the Alabama delegation, and especially through our family that the level of excitement was truly indescribable.

Minutes away from airtime, thousands of people were still milling around near their seats, looking for friends and making final predictions about who might win. From the stage the live audience was being briefed about what would happen during television commercial breaks and where to watch monitors for cues on when to applaud.

About that time I leaned over toward Heather's grandpa and whispered, "I can't believe I'm not nervous. You know what an emotional wreck I always am the final night of a pageant. It makes me wonder if something is wrong."

Granddad Gray grinned back at me. "It's only because things haven't started yet. Don't worry. You'll be a basket case soon enough! The show's about to begin."

I grinned back at him and sat back upright in my seat thinking, *He's probably right.* I was sure I was about to be hit with the worst case of nerves in pageant history.

But that next moment the strangest sensation came over me. A river of warmth started at the top of my head and flowed all the way down through my body and out the tips of my toes. And in my mind, as clear as day, I heard a voice saying, *Relax and enjoy. Tonight is hers.*

I didn't breathe a word to anyone about what I'd just felt and heard. I didn't dare. Besides, there wasn't time.

That's when the orchestra began and the live pageant broadcast went on the air around the country. And around the world.

For most of those next three hours I was able to *relax and enjoy* that Miss America Pageant like no other pageant Heather had been in before. I grew a little anxious when it was time for that onstage interview with Regis Philbin in front of those 13,000 people packed into the convention center and millions more clustered in front of television sets around the world. And then there was that nerve-wracking

wait through the final commercial break and the slow announcement of fourth . . . third . . . and second runners-up.

To tell you the truth, I didn't exactly *relax* when Regis said, "And the new Miss America 1995, Miss Alabama, Heather Whitestone!"

But I certainly did *enjoy* those next few minutes as I watched my grown-up daughter take her long walk out on that same slick runway again by herself this time, wearing a crown and waving to the world.

It wasn't until I'd been ushered backstage and was sitting—with Stacey, Melissa, and my parents— in Heather's first official press conference as Miss America that I remembered the message I'd received and thought, *Heather's dream* has *come true. Tonight* is *hers!*

When the last parties ended long after midnight, Heather and I stepped into her hotel suite bedroom to talk. As the door closed behind us and we were alone together for the first time in months, we looked at each other and exclaimed, almost in unison: "Do you believe this!"

Sitting together on the edge of her bed, Heather began to tell me about all the telegrams she'd gotten that week wishing her well. "Sandi Patty sent one! And I got another one from . . ." and she excitedly ran off a long list.

When she wound down a little I decided I had to

tell someone, so I said to her, "The strangest thing happened to me tonight, Heather. You know how I'm always such a nervous wreck before pageants?"

She nodded. She knew me well.

"Well, tonight I wasn't the least bit nervous. And just before we went on the air, this strange warmth just washed over me, and it was like I heard a voice saying, 'Relax and enjoy. Tonight is hers!'"

Heather got the strangest look on her face. "You're not going to believe this, Mother. But just before the pageant started tonight, I was standing backstage when this strange warmth passed through my body and I heard a voice say, 'Relax and dance for me tonight.' And I wasn't a bit nervous all night!"

I don't know how Heather felt at that moment. But as we looked at each other in silent awe, I felt chills running up and down my spine.

And it wasn't because my daughter had just been crowned Miss America.

12

Anything Is Possible!

Of course, September 17, 1994, was just the beginning of the fulfillment of Heather's Miss America dream.

In the first twenty-four hours after Heather was crowned, the Miss America Organization received over 3,000 requests for her personal appearances. Within two days the incredible volume of incoming correspondence burned up their fax machine, and the office had to hire eight new people just to handle Heather's mail.

By the end of the first month of her reign, Heather had already been granted a personal audience with the president of the United States, met twice with the First Lady, and launched her official platform "Anything Is Possible!" in a Capitol Hill press conference accompanied by the Alabama congressional delegation. President Clinton appointed Heather to his Executive Committee for Employment of People with Disabilities. She also met with the U.S. Secretary of Education to discuss ways she could work with his department over the coming year.

Many national publications ran features on the new Miss America. And Heather crisscrossed the country several times making thousands of public appearances and speaking to a wide variety of audiences.

The public response to Heather and her message of inspiration and hope has been absolutely mind-boggling. Within four months Heather had received more requests for personal appearances than any other Miss America in history.

Already my daughter has had a positive effect on many lives. I've heard from countless people who want to tell me how inspired they have been by Heather's story and by her message of acceptance, encouragement, and hope. I love receiving letters from kids who say that Heather's "Anything Is Possible!" campaign has shown them they don't have to be limited by their handicaps. Or as one physically handicapped girl wrote Heather, "Since you spoke here, for the first time ever, I feel accepted at my school."

Another one of my favorite letters came from a mother who wrote to say her young daughter had wanted to dress up as Miss America for Halloween. So the mother had gotten her a pretty dress, created a crown, and even made the girl a little scepter. But when her mother got her dressed and put her in front of a mirror, the little girl wasn't happy at all. "What's wrong?" her mother asked. "Everything is perfect!"

"No!" replied the little girl. "Miss America has a hearing aid." And she wouldn't go out trick-or-treating until her mother had fashioned a cardboard hearing aid she could wear to look like the *real* Miss America.

Not everyone has been so accepting of Heather and the way she has dealt with her deafness. Many people in the deaf community criticized Heather for using speech rather than sign during most of her public appearances as Miss America. They accused her of selling out to the hearing world.

I think Heather was surprised and a little hurt by their criticism. But I wasn't surprised. When Heather was a little girl and I was trying to decide how we would teach her to communicate, I learned how people argued and fought over the question of oral speech versus sign language. But it saddens me that these same arguments are still happening today, twenty years later.

And I'm sorry Heather has been caught in the middle of these arguments. But I am very proud of the way she's been willing to take the criticism and still try to share her message in the deaf community.

My prayer is that people—both hearing and deaf—will see Heather for who she is. I want them to see that as Miss America, she can pursue an even more worthy dream—to be a bridge between our two worlds so that both hearing and deaf people will have a better understanding and appreciation for each other.

I think this is happening. I know that as Miss America's mom I receive many invitations to speak. And whenever I speak to school groups, I tell them that one of the most important lessons to be learned from Heather's story is to realize that every one of us has our own strengths and weaknesses. Those are the things that make us each unique.

Sometimes we get so discouraged by our weaknesses that we fail to discover and use our strengths. But God has carefully and thoughtfully given each of us some strengths we can use for him. Sometimes our strengths may not be obvious. But they are always there.

True friends help us find and develop those strengths. True friends also help us face, accept, and overcome our weaknesses.

One of the big reasons I have written this book

about my daughter is to help people realize that we don't have to be limited by our handicaps and our weaknesses. With God's help, a "limitation" can be the very thing that makes us a unique person he can use in a very special way.

All of Heather's life so many people only saw the "limitations." But God saw the possibilities. And he helped me to see them as well.

So many times during this year of Heather's reign I've thought of my dreams for her, how even though I always told her, "Yes, you can, Heather. Anything is possible!" the reality of all that has happened is almost too much to believe. Some days I've almost had to pinch myself to make sure it is all truly happening.

Then I see my daughter's face on the cover of a national magazine, I hear her familiar voice on the radio, or I watch her being interviewed on network television, and I realize both our dreams have come true.

There she is, Miss America!